I0116197

Dinesh D'Souza's
WHAT'S SO GREAT ABOUT AMERICA:
A Reply, Refutation and Rebuttal

DINESH D'SOUZA'S

WHAT'S SO GREAT ABOUT AMERICA

A REPLY, REFUTATION AND REBUTTAL

BY

HAROLD PALMER

TIME 🏛 BOOKS

Dinesh D'Souza's
WHAT'S SO GREAT ABOUT AMERICA:
A Reply, Refutation and Rebuttal

© 2016 by TellerBooks™. All rights reserved. No part of this publication may be reproduced or transmitted in any form or by any means, including photocopying, recording, or copying to any storage and retrieval system, without express written permission from the copyright holder.

ISBN (13) (Paperback): 978-1-68109-019-1
ISBN (10) (Paperback): 1-68109-019-8
ISBN (13) (Kindle): 978-1-68109-020-7
ISBN (10) (Kindle): 1-68109-020-1
ISBN (13) (ePub): 978-1-68109-021-4
ISBN (10) (ePub): 1-68109-021-X

Time Books™
an imprint of TellerBooks™
TellerBooks.com/Time_Books

t TellerBooks

www.TellerBooks.com

Manufactured in the U.S.A.

DISCLAIMER: The opinions, views, positions and conclusions expressed in this volume reflect those of the individual author and not necessarily those of the publisher or any of its imprints, editors or employees.

ABOUT THE IMPRINT

The *Reply, Refutation and Rebuttal* Series™ of Time Books™ publishes monographs and treatises that reply to contemporary perspectives on political, philosophical and religious issues.

Complete your collection with the following titles:

- Dinesh D'Souza's *What's So Great About America*: A Reply, Refutation and Rebuttal
- Dr. Gregory Boyd's *Myth of a Christian Nation:* A Reply, Refutation and Rebuttal
- Dr. Mel White's *What the Bible Says and Doesn't Say About Homosexuality*: A Reply, Refutation and Rebuttal
- Dr. H. M. Baagil's *Muslim-Christian Dialogue*: A Reply, Refutation and Rebuttal
- *The Communist Manifesto* of Karl Marx and Friedrich Engels: A Reply, Refutation and Rebuttal

TIME 🏛 BOOKS

The mission of Time Books™ is to reintroduce time-tested values and truths to modern debates on political, economic, and moral issues. The imprint focuses on books and monographs dealing with society, ethics, and public policy.

CONTENTS

CHAPTER 1. OVERVIEW

Is America a nation like any other, with a past marked by injustice and oppression? Or is America a shining city on a hill, marked by exceptionalism, one where the lamp of liberty and democracy burns brightly? Dinesh D'Souza has written *What's So Great About America* to respond to America's critics, who "deny that there is anything unique about America" (p. 162). These critics include "multiculturalists who allege historical racism and the ongoing oppression of minorities; ... Third World intellectuals who deplore the legacy of colonialism; ... Western leftists who see America as a force for evil in the world; and ... Islamic fundamentalists and cultural conservatives who view America as culturally decadent and morally degenerate" (p. 163). In answering these critics, D'Souza argues that America is not only good, but that it is a great nation marked by exceptionalism and the vindication of values universal to mankind.

To execute a successful book, D'Souza must refute the accounts of America's critics on three points key to their argument: (i) America's oppression of the Native Americans; (ii) slavery; and (iii) historic discrimination of African Americans and other minorities. Finally, in order to refute the criticisms of cultural conservatives who deplore America as "culturally decadent and morally degenerate," he must prove that American society is, despite its appearance, a virtuous society.

D'Souza makes a strong case for America, arguing that it is a free and prosperous society with unlimited opportunity for those seeking a better life. Yet despite his enthusiasm for America, his treatment of America's "sins," each of which is further discussed below, is inadequate, one-sided and does not result in the vindication of America from the claims of her critics.

CHAPTER 2. SLAVERY IN AMERICA

I. SLAVERY WAS RAMPANT ALL OVER THE WORLD

A. D'Souza's Argument

Dinesh D'Souza begins to excuse the practice of slavery in early America on the basis that slavery was so rampant around the world that it was at the time not contrary to then-prevailing notions of morality. D'Souza writes (p. 111):

> For millennia, slavery was an accepted part of society. In numerous civilizations both Western and non-Western, slavery needed no defenders because it had no critics. The major religions of the world, including Christianity and Islam, permitted slavery ... But starting in the seventeenth century, certain segments of Christianity—initially the Quakers, then the evangelical Christians—began to interpret biblical equality as forbidding the ownership of one man by another. Only then, for the first time, did slavery become a political problem.

D'Souza traces the view of slavery's "normalcy" to Aristotle, for whom conventional slavery, while perhaps unjust, was expedient.

B. Palmer's Reply

Before addressing the flaw in D'Souza's argument, it should be noted that centuries before slavery became a "political problem" in nineteenth-century America, other countries (*e.g.*, Iceland in 1117; Russia in 1723 (retaining only serfdom)) voluntarily abolished slavery. Moreover, when slavery became a "political problem" in the nineteenth century, the United States was one of the last of the Western nations to abolish it. Excluding non-Western Muslim countries, only Cuba (1886) and Brazil (1888) abolished slavery after the United States did. Nations that abolished slavery earlier than the United States include Haiti (1804), Uruguay (1814), Portugal (1818), Spain (1818), Mexico (1820), Colombia (1821), Greece (1822), Chile (1823), Boliva (1821), British Empire (1838), Sweden (1847), France (1848) (freeing slaves in all of its colonies and founding Gabon for their resettlement), Argentina (1853), Peru (1854) and Venezuela (1854). Moreover, unlike the United States, which fought the bloodiest war in its history to abolish slavery, most of the other nations that abolished slavery did so peacefully.

One thus sees that abolitionism did not appear in a vacuum in nineteenth-century America. Rather, it had been an ongoing international affair, with America as one of the last Western nations to abolish the practice. Yet even if slavery were widely accepted around the world at the time of its abolition in America, America would be no less guilty of participating in the oppressive practice.

In the modern world, many studies continue to raise the flag on contemporary practices such as human trafficking and indentured servitude that strongly resemble historic slavery. The United Nations and non-governmental organizations estimate that between 10 million to 30 million people remain trapped in non-institutional slavery today. The fact that this is widespread or common does not make it any less shameful or sinful. In other words, the widespread nature of a practice in the twentieth century should make it any more acceptable in the twentieth century than it did in the nineteenth century.

II. THE "THREE-FIFTHS" CLAUSE WAS ANTISLAVERY IN ITS NATURE

A. D'Souza's Argument

Dinesh D'Souza cites leading black scholar John Hope Franklin to frame the argument against the founders (p. 108-09):

> [They wrote] eloquently at one moment for the brotherhood of man and in the next moment denied it to their black brothers ... by equating five black men with three white men ... Having created a tragically flawed revolutionary doctrine and a Constitution that did not bestow the blessings of liberty on its posterity, the founding fathers set the stage for every succeeding generation to ... temporize on those principles of liberty that were supposed to be the very foundation of our system of government.

D'Souza counters Franklin by arguing that the "three-fifths" clause actually "has nothing to say about the intrinsic worth of blacks" (p. 109). He writes (p. 109-10):

> The origins of the clause are to be found in the debate between the northern states and the southern states over the issue of political representation. The South wanted to count blacks as whole persons, in order to increase its political power. The North wanted blacks to count for nothing—not of the purpose of rejecting their humanity, but in order to preserve and strengthen the antislavery majority in Congress. It was not a proslavery southerner but an antislavery northerner, James Wilson of Pennsylvania, who proposed the three-fifths comprise. The effect was to limit the South's political representation and its ability to protect the institution of slavery. Frederick Douglass understood this: he called the three-fifths clause 'a downright disability laid upon the slaveholding states' which deprived them of 'two-fifths of their natural basis of representation.'

For D'Souza, the "three-fifths" clause is thus a provision of the Constitution that was anti-slavery rather than pro-slavery in its nature. Therefore, it cannot be used as evidence that the Constitution condoned slavery.

B. Palmer's Reply

Regardless of the intent of the "three-fifths" clause, its impact was to degrade the value of African American slaves. If two men are equal, a law may not equate one of them as having the same value as three fifths of the other. If the founders were true to their words, they would have gone beyond lip service to equality and actually treated all men as equal, giving them equal rights to vote. If all men, black or white, free or slave, were given equal rights, there would have been no need for the three-fifths clause because most or all of the slaves would have voted to abolish slavery, obviating the need to diminish the congressional representation of southern States.

III.IMPRACTICALITY OF FREEING ALL OF THE SLAVES IMMEDIATELY

A. D'Souza's Argument

Dinesh D'Souza highlights the impracticality of freeing all slaves immediately at the American founding and giving them full rights. He writes that the founders recognized the degraded condition of black Americans and understood it posed a "formidable hurdle to granting blacks the rights of citizenship" (p. 113). However, unlike monarchies and aristocracies, which only require subjects to obey, "self-government requires citizens who have the capacity to be rulers. Jefferson and the founders were legitimately concerned that a group that had been enslaved for centuries was not ready to assume the responsibility of democratic self-rule" (p. 113). Therefore, the degraded condition of blacks in America prevented them from being granted citizenship in a democratic society.

B. Palmer's Reply

The impracticality of abolishing slavery cannot be used to justify the continuation of slavery. It did not impede abolition in other nations, such as Portugal (1818), Spain (1818), Colombia (1821), Greece (1822), the British Empire (1838), Sweden (1847), France (1848) or Venezuela (1854). So why should it impede abolition in America, which is for D'Souza "greater" than these other nations?

D'Souza's response is there was a special impediment in the case of America: Unlike monarchies and aristocracies, which only require subjects to obey, America was a democracy, and "self-government requires citizens who have the capacity to be rulers" (p. 113). If the founders emancipated all of the slaves, a people that had been subject to abuse and prejudice for centuries, they would not get along well in a land that required its citizens to take on the special responsibilities of self-rule.

If this were true, one is left wondering why America was able to abolish slavery in 1865 but not in 1776? Was America any less democratic in 1865 than it was in 1776? Did it require any less civic duty of its citizens in 1865 than it did in 1776? The irony in D'Souza's argument is that he draws on the democratic form of government, which purportedly protects *more* freedoms than those of America's then-contemporary European counterparts, as the reason that America could not so readily abolish slavery and vindicate slaves' rights.

Is D'Souza's argument valid? The fundamental difference between the monarchies of Europe and the American republic is not that America required its citizens to self-rule; rather, America gave its citizens the *right* to self-rule. The right was one that citizens could choose to exercise; no one was ever required to exercise the right to vote, to peacefully assemble or to petition the government for a redress of grievances. An American's exercise of his constitutionally-guaranteed rights is his own choice. Living as a freed slave granted citizenship in America would be no more challenging or difficult than living as a freed slave in Europe; both obligate him to obey the laws, but only the free democracy gives him the option to exercise certain rights.

Yet even if D'Souza were correct on the impracticality of freeing the slaves, the solution would not be to continue slavery into perpetuity; rather, it would be gradual emancipation, through, for example, liberating future children of slaves or slaves that reach a certain age; undertaking a system of compensated emancipation or forced apprenticeship; granting freed slaves land and tools to work land; or repatriating slaves to Africa.

IV. THE FRAMERS' DILEMMA: HOW TO UPHOLD DEMOCRACY AND YET ABOLISH SLAVERY

A. D'Souza's Argument

Dinesh D'Souza goes on to argue that the founders were in a difficult dilemma with respect to the abolition of slavery. On the one hand, they wanted to frame a system of governance by popular consent. On the other hand, there was not enough support among white Americans to support the abolition of slavery. Therefore, the only way to have abolished slavery would have been through compromising popular consent that was necessary to true democracy. D'Souza writes that "[t]o outlaw slavery without the consent of the majority of whites would be to destroy democracy, indeed to destroy the very basis for outlawing slavery itself" (p. 114). He continues (p. 116):

> The principle of popular rule is based on Jefferson's doctrine that 'all men are created equal,' yet the greatest crisis in American history arose when the people denied that 'all men are created equal' and in so doing denied the basis of their own legitimacy. Lincoln had two choices: work to overthrow democracy, or work to secure consent through persuasion.

B. Palmer's Reply

The flaw in D'Souza's argument is that it is operating from the perspective that only the white man's vote counts in a democracy. Because only white men have the right to exercise rights guaranteed in a democratic society—including the right to consent to their government and to vote for their leaders, the founders were unable to abolish slavery through popular consent since the majority of white Americans supported slavery.

What happens to this argument from an equal-rights point of view? All men are created equal, and all have certain unalienable rights endowed by their creator. All men have access to these rights, including the right to self-governance and to choose one's governors, regardless of their skin color. If this view were adopted, then there would be no tension between abolition and the consent of the governed. With over half a million African Americans constituting America's population at the time of the founding, blacks constituting nearly 20% of the total US population would have tipped the balance in favor of abolition without having ever undermining democracy consent. This argument only fails if we begin from the starting point that blacks should not be given the right to vote to begin with, a stand that is inconsistent with the principles promulgated by the founders in the Declaration of Independence.

V. THE CONSTITUTION WAS NEUTRAL ON THE QUESTION OF SLAVERY

A. D'Souza's Argument

In his final point about slavery, D'Souza contends that the founders did not draft a constitution that institutes, legitimizes or condones slavery; rather, the Constitution was neutral on the question of slavery. Because of the sensitivity of the political question of slavery at the time, and the necessity of building enough support to establish a union, the founders left the question of slavery up to the States and out of the Constitution, which never even mentions the institution by name. D'Souza quotes Frederick Douglass, who "once denounced the Constitution but who eventually reached the conclusion that it contained antislavery principles," and who said, "Abolish slavery tomorrow, and not a sentence or syllable of the Constitution needs to be altered" (p. 117).

B. Palmer's Reply

If the Constitution really were neutral on slavery, there would have been no need for the post-Civil War Thirteenth, Fourteenth and Fifteenth Amendments (abolishing slavery, establishing citizenship rights, and granting suffrage to blacks, respectively). If slavery were not recognized in the Constitution, there would be no need for any of these amendments. Congress or the President could have simply enforced the rights granted in the Constitution, interpreting them as applicable to all people, regardless of race.

Of course, amending to the Constitution was necessary because of its implicit recognition of slavery by distinguishing between "free persons" and "all other persons" and providing guidance on counting slaves for the purpose of political representation. Amending the Constitution was therefore a necessary step in the abolition of slavery, and shows that the founders, in instituting a constitution that implicitly legitimized slavery, compromised on the lofty principles they promulgated in the Declaration of Independence.

CHAPTER 3. AMERICA'S TREATMENT OF THE NATIVE AMERICANS, RACISM AND MORAL CORRUPTION

I. AMERICA'S TREATMENT OF THE NATIVE AMERICANS

A. D'Souza's Argument

Dinesh D'Souza begins by outlining the claims made by American Indians against America. "It is commonplace among American Indians that the white man arrived on these shores with an incorrigible bigotry toward native peoples and then put into effect a policy of exterminating the Indian population. If 'America' represents a country that is guilty of unmitigated hatred and genocide, how can the native Indians who were victims of this viciousness and slaughter be expected to salute the flag?" (p. 105).

Yet D'Souza argues that "[e]ven on the count of racism against Indians, the evidence is ambiguous" (p. 105). For example, Thomas Jefferson, "while entertaining doubts that blacks were as intelligent as whites, ... confidently stated that any backwardness on the part of the Indian was entirely the result of circumstance" (p. 105). Jefferson and other leading figures proposed intermarriage between whites and Native Americans to integrate them into the mainstream (p. 106).

D'Souza then sets off to debunk the claim that the European settlers were guilty of genocide. While "millions of Indians perished as a result of contact with the white man, … for the most part they died by contracting his diseases: smallpox, measles, malaria, tuberculosis" (p. 106). The white man generally transmitted diseases to the Indians without knowing it and the Indians "died in large number s because they had not developed immunities" (p. 106). The white settlers cannot therefore be charged with genocide because they did not intend to wipe out the Indian population.

B. Palmer's Reply

The fact that the early settlers were not guilty of genocide does not mean that they were not guilty of other wrongdoing. D'Souza concedes that that none of his stated arguments excuse "the settlers' injustices" or diminishes "the historical misfortunate of the American Indians" (p. 106). However, rather than giving these injustices substantial treatment, D'Souza merely mentions them in passing. This, in contrast to the long apologetic that D'Souza gives in defense of the settlers and the founders, undermines the book's objectivity.

II. RACISM

A. D'Souza's Argument

After his treatment of slavery, D'Souza tackles the question of racism. He first frames the argument of affirmative activists: Racial preferences are indispensable because of the pervasiveness of racism and discrimination in American society. Yet when D'Souza asks affirmative activists if they know of any bigots in admissions offices trying to keep blacks and Hispanics out, his question has never led to the identification of bigots (p. 119). The activists counter that discrimination is more subtle, through such "racially and culturally biased" institutions as the Scholastic Assessment Test (SAT) (p. 119).

Dinesh D'Souza replies to this criticism by showing that if the SAT were biased, this would show up on the verbal section rather than on the math section, since no one can credibly argue that algebra or equations can be racially biased. Yet the gap between whites and blacks is greater on the math section than on the verbal section. For D'Souza, then, the difference is attributable not to racism but to merit, which is "the primary obstacle to enrolling larger numbers of blacks and Hispanics in selective universities" (p. 121). He further shows that across the board, on all objective tests, whites and Asians do the best, followed by Hispanics and African-Americans at the bottom (p. 120).

Martin Luther King, Jr. demanded equality of rights for individuals in America. This will, however, naturally lead to unequal representation of certain ethnic groups in certain professions over others. Consider the NBA, which selects players based on merit. It is dominated by black players, yet no one calls for affirmative action to place more Jews and Asians in the NBA. Similarly, society should not call for affirmative action to place more blacks and Hispanics at America's elite schools.

Next, D'Souza goes on to examine some of the causes for the discrepancy in merit between racial groups, with whites and Asians at the top and blacks on the bottom. He cities a study by Sanford Dornbusch, which found (p. 126):

> Asian -American students devote relatively more time to their studies, are more likely to attribute their success to hard work, and are more likely to report that their parents have high standards for school performance ... In contrast, African American and Hispanic students are more cavalier about the consequences of poor school performance, devote less time to their studies, are less likely than others to attribute their success to hard work, and report that their parents have relatively lower standards.

As for why Asian Americans and African Americans display these differences in behavior, D'Souza highlights the two-parent household. Whereas the illegitimacy rate in the Asian-American community is less than 5%, it is nearly 70% in the African American community. Parents in Asian American communities are therefore able to devote more time to their children, in contrast with African-American families where a single parent often struggles alone.

Some argue that the single-family African-American household is the modern fruit of the sin of slavery, which tore apart families and sold off children and spouses as commercial property. However, D'Souza points out that from the early twentieth century through the 1965, the illegitimacy rate for blacks in the US ranged from 20% to 25%. However, "it is during the period from 1965 to the present—a period that saw the Great Society, the civil rights law, affirmative action, welfare, and other attempts to integrate blacks into the mainstream and raise their standard of living—that the black family disintegrated" (p. 127). This disintegration cannot be blamed on racism or on discrimination, because African-American families in the early twentieth century that experienced more racism, poverty and unemployment than their modern counterparts, yet more often stayed together as cohesive family units.

B. Palmer's Reply

Dinesh D'Souza's argument on racism is well-researched, conceived and articulated. However, it is flawed in one respect. Regardless of whether the under-achievement of African Americans today is due to merit, as D'Souza maintains, or racism and discrimination, as affirmative activists maintain, the fact is that discrimination based on skin color is a black blotch on American history that the book skims over.

D'Souza argues that the plight of blacks in America today is largely the consequence of their own doing. Regardless of whether this is true, the plight of blacks in American until 1964 was the consequence of factors outside of their control: discrimination by white-controlled restaurants, banks, common carriers and schools that deprived of full participation in American civic life. African Americans were segregated in and discriminated against by universities and employers. Even John Hope Franklin, the renowned historian, was despite his Harvard Ph.D. and other extensive qualifications told that he was the "wrong color" when volunteering to join the US Navy in World War II.

This great black blotch on America's past calls into question D'Souza's central thesis that America is a "great." His thesis would have been stronger had he devoted more attention not to the state of America today, but to America's past sins and showing how America, while its treatment of slaves and minorities may have been as unjust as that of other nations, can still be called "great."

III. AMERICA'S MORALLY-DECADENT CULTURE

A. D'Souza's Argument

On a final note, D'Souza treats criticisms coming from culturally conservative and Islamic circles. On the Islamic front, he discusses Sayyid Qutb's argument, which holds that America's achievements in securing freedom for her people are trivial, because it is virtue, not freedom, that is supreme. D'Souza writes (p. 86):

> Qutb would not be impressed by New York's great productivity or its varied cuisine or the fact that people of different backgrounds get along together. He would dismiss all that as worthless triviality. He makes his argument on the highest level. In the good society, he contends, it is God, and not man, who rules. God is the source of all authority, including legitimate political authority. Virtue, not freedom, is the highest value. Therefore God's commands, not man's laws, should govern the society. The goal of the regime is to make people better, not to make them better off.

While Qutb's argument "falls harshly on American ears," it is essentially the same argument made by Plato and the classical philosophers, "who argued that the best regime is devoted to inculcating virtue" (p. 86). D'Souza concedes that while this sounds commendable in principle, Plato's *Republic* is not an actual city; it is a utopian picture that even Plato did not expect to see realized. He then gives examples of theocracies such as Afghanistan under the Taliban and the Islamic Republic of Iran, which are purportedly ruled by God but "seem to be characterized by widespread misery, discontent, tyranny, and inequality" (p. 87).

D'Souza concludes: "Is God, then, such an incompetent ruler?" (p. 87).

B. Palmer's Reply

While showing the shortfalls in the implementation of a theocratic society, D'Souza fails to defend America's decadent culture or deal with the fact that moral decay in recent years undermines America's greatness. Rather, he agrees with America's conservative and Islamic critics, so much so that he does not want his daughter to be "Americanized" (p. 99) and is instead "constantly battling to shield [her] from toxic influences in American culture that threaten to destroy her innocence" (p. 34).

CHAPTER 4. CONCLUSION

This book would have been more credible if it argued for America's merits while admitting her faults. Instead, it is a shiny, propaganda-like account of America. The prophet Joel wrote that a nation will not receive God's blessing until it comes before Him in repentance. We see this principle further illustrated in the parable of the Pharisee and the Publican. We as Americans should recognize that we will not get very far by emulating the Pharisee's proud boasting. It was the tax collector, who acknowledging his sin, cried out for God's mercy and went home justified (Luke 18:11-14). Let us emulate the tax collector, collectively recognizing the sins of our past and crying out to God in repentance. Only then can we perfect our nation and carve out a future where every individual's right to life, liberty and the pursuit of happiness is vindicated.

www.ingramcontent.com/pod-product-compliance
Lightning Source LLC
Chambersburg PA
CBHW060532280326
41933CB00014B/3141